SURVIVING THE RING:

EXPERT ADVICE FOR GETTING IN AND STAYING IN THE TOUGH WORLD OF PRO WRESTLING

Jeff "The Ref" Coles

Published by: JTR Publishing

© Copyright 2014. Jeff Coles. All rights reserved. This book contains material protected under International and Federal Copyright Laws and Treaties. Any unauthorized reprint or use of this material is prohibited. No part of this book may be reproduced or transmitted in any form or by any means, electronic or mechanical, including photocopying, recording, scanning or by any information storage and retrieval system without express written permission from the author and/or the publisher.

ISBN: 978-0692252338

Disclaimer:

This book is presented solely for educational purposes. The author and publisher are not offering it as legal or other professional services advice. While best efforts have been used in preparing this book, the author and publisher make no representations or warranties of any kind, and assume no liabilities of any kind with respect to the accuracy or completeness of the contents. The author and publisher specifically disclaim any implied warranties of merchantability or fitness of use for a particular purpose.

Neither the author nor the publisher shall be held liable or responsible to any person or entity with respect to any loss or incidental or consequential damages caused, or alleged to have been caused, directly or indirectly, by the information or strategies contained herein, as the advice and strategies contained herein may not be suitable for your own unique situation. You should seek the services of a competent professional before beginning any strategy or taking any action.

DEDICATION

I remember exactly where I was Sunday night, April 1, 1990. I was enrolled at Kent State University and lived in Terrace Hall (it's a shame that building doesn't exist anymore). Since my roommate and I -- who were both huge wrestling fans -- were penniless students, we couldn't go to the bar to watch the WrestleMania VI pay-per-view.

So we stayed on campus, hoping the news would say something about the outcome of the main event: Hulk Hogan versus the Ultimate Warrior for the WWF Championship. I was pulling for Hogan since he had been my idol for years, but I just couldn't go against the Warrior.

Unfortunately, the news said nothing about the match. I guess it was more important to discuss the Cleveland Indians and Cavaliers failing to win than report on a "fake" sports event that drew over 70,000 people to the Sky Dome in Toronto. Shortly after I switched the channel, one of our friends came running into the room.

"George Michael's Sports Machine has the results of the match!" he yelled. "They're going to give it after the commercials!"

I turned on the channel and caught the lead-in by Michaels: "Let's go to the Sky Dome in Toronto. And folks, this is no April Fools' joke. The Ultimate Warrior has ***cleanly*** pinned and defeated Hulk Hogan for the WWF Championship!"

I was stunned...shocked...and looked at the television with my mouth wide open. My mind was blank, and I was speechless because I couldn't believe what I had just heard: "***Cleanly*** pinned!"

No swerve. No "evil twin" referee. No Million Dollar Man buyout. No run-ins. Just a missed leg drop, an Ultimate splash, and in only three seconds my hero had been cleanly vanquished and without dispute.

It was almost as if someone had died, and the way I was feeling I thought it was me. All I had wanted was to see was the match between these two epic titans that was appropriately tagged "The Ultimate Challenge." But unfortunately I hadn't been at the bar to witness this history-making event.

Months later I got my hands on a VHS copy of WrestleMania VI from a video store (remember those?). I remember hearing the pre-match promos from both wrestlers, but the Warrior's was different. Hogan's adversaries claimed they were "gonna take the WWF title and destroy Hulkamania!"

But the Ultimate Warrior said something in the promo I had never heard a Hogan opponent say: "I come not to destroy Hulkamania, but to unite the Maniacs and the Warriors as one." Wow! Talk about respect. This guy wasn't trying to end anything; he was trying to start something -- a merging of the two most "powerful forces" in the WWF.

I sat on the couch and immersed myself in that match. I felt every move, bump, chop, kick, punch, and clothesline. I watched intently as Hogan fell to the outside, favoring his knee.

I heard him tell the referee, "It's gone, brother. My knee's gone." Whether it was or not, I really can't say. All I know is the match continued and I got to see it all.

Then came the finish I had waited for months to see: "Warrior with the gorilla press slam, the splash. One...two...Hogan kicks out and he is fired up! Three punches to Warrior, whip off the ropes, the Big Boot! Hogan goes up for the leg drop. Warrior moved! Hogan is down. Warrior off the ropes...the big splash! He could have him! One...two...three! The Warrior has done it!"

The win was legit. While that was emotional enough, what happened post-match was something that will live with me forever. Hogan -- dejected and exhausted -- lumbered over to the timekeeper's table and picked up what used to be his title belt. As he slowly climbed back into the ring, a hush filled the Sky Dome as people were wondering what the Hulk was going to do.

Hogan walked up to Warrior and presented him with the WWF Heavyweight Championship. Warrior took the belt and the two embraced in the center of the ring. The torch had officially been passed, and Warrior had solidified his legacy.

Being a young dreamer and wrestling hopeful I wept not for Hulk's loss, but because of the class and dignity he showed his opponent in defeat.

And things had indeed begun to change in the world of pro wrestling.

The image of Warrior holding both the WWF Championship and the Intercontinental Championship high in the air as the pyro went off behind him was something to behold. He turned, looked at the entranceway and locked eyes with Hogan. Then he pointed a finger at him and slammed his massive fist over his heart, signaling to the world, "You're the man, Hogan!"

Hogan mirrored the gesture, almost as if to say, "It's all yours now, brother. Run with it." (I can feel the tears welling up as I remember what I felt while watching their interactions.)

* * * * * * *

I also remember where I was Tuesday night, April 8, 2014. I was training with the Honor Pro boys in Scottsdale, Arizona. Some trainees were being coached in the ring, a few were building a new entrance ramp, and the rest were on their phones.

Around 9:00 p.m. I heard someone yell "Dude! Warrior just died! He collapsed in front of his wife!"

Dead silence.

Then almost in unison we all yelled, "**_BULLSHIT!_**"

Within seconds we were all on our phones Googling, Facebooking, trying to get some answers about what happened to the Warrior. Where was he? What happened? Were his kids with them? Were they still in New Orleans?

My God, what the hell just happened? As reported, Warrior collapsed at a Scottsdale hotel (not far from us) while walking to his car with his wife, and was pronounced dead at the hospital.

This was truly serendipitous, because WWE had released a DVD called "The Self-Destruction of the Ultimate Warrior," which all but destroyed Warrior's legendary career. He wasn't included in the original discussions, so WWE basically created a smear campaign. Various superstars talked about how hard he was to work with, how stiff he worked, how he was an egomaniac, and wanted "Hogan money" for less work. Triple H completely buried Warrior on that DVD.

Sure, Warrior had been outspoken on many topics, and had made many enemies because of his opinions and perceptions. He had lashed out at Ted DiBiase for becoming a born-again Christian, Jake Roberts when he was trying to get clean and sober, and even Hulk Hogan for various reasons. I couldn't understand why he was so uber-critical of these other guys, especially when most were no longer working.

It seemed like Warrior had burned every bridge he had in wrestling, but then something happened. A "resurgence" of his career, if that's what you want to call it.

WWE and Warrior started talking again, because it appeared his fans were wanting him to reappear. The WWE 2K14 videogame could be preordered, which included the Ultimate Warrior as a playable character. This opened the door for more talks between WWE and Warrior for some kind of return to pro wrestling.

WWE and Warrior worked together to produce "The Ultimate Collection," a Blu-Ray/DVD compilation of Warrior's greatest matches, as well as sit-down interviews with Warrior which had never happened before. Plus it set the record straight by saying, "To tell the REAL truth of the Ultimate Warrior."

With the new influx of "Warrior-ness" there was only one more logical step: He became immortal when he was inducted into the WWE Hall of Fame on Saturday, April 5, 2014 (the URL link to the YouTube video can be found in Resources). This was monumental, mainly because of the bad history between him and Vince McMahon, the owner of WWE. There's so much that went on behind the scenes that I don't want to get into it. Let's just say that Warrior being acknowledged was nothing short of miraculous.

I personally believe his induction into the Hall of Fame served two fundamental purposes. First, he deserved to be there. Warrior had pinned the most iconic superstar of all time (Hulk Hogan). He simultaneously held the only two WWF singles titles. He had beat Andre the Giant in 30 seconds, and "retired" Macho Man Randy Savage. Warrior was the reason WWF continued to grow after Hogan left. In just a few years he had moved mountains, defeated legends, and kept freaking going!

Second, there was a lot of bad blood between Warrior and the people I mentioned earlier. Ironically, all of them were at the Hall of Fame ceremony. Jake Roberts and Scott Hall were also being inducted, as well as Hulk Hogan who served as the "host" of WrestleMania XXX.

I can only speculate how their initial meetings went, but the end result was that a lot of fences were mended. I've seen pictures and videos of Hulk and Warrior shaking hands and embracing, and he and Jake doing the same. There's even a photo of Warrior and Vince McMahon hugging each other and grinning from ear to ear. In addition, there were comments on Facebook from these men who all basically said it felt good to finally bury the hatchet and move forward as friends.

(NOTE: I highly recommend watching Warrior's emotional Hall of Fame acceptance speech as he speaks from the heart. He really wanted everyone to know that wasn't a bad guy, and that he just wanted to be happy with his life. You can find the URL link in Resources.)

The next day at WrestleMania XXX, all of the HOF inductees came out to wave and acknowledge the crowd…except one.

Then, I heard the riff, the same theme music I had heard so many times that signified it was time to prepare for a trip to parts unknown. The Warrior's famous quote, "Load up the spaceship…with the rocket fuel…!" suddenly came to mind as my heart raced and the goosebumps returned.

It had been 24 years since his greatest victory with Hulk Hogan. Instead of being the young wrestling hopeful of 1990, I was now a 43-year-old man with nothing but memories of the Warrior's battles both in and out of the ring, and he was finally getting his due. And for that one precious moment I was full of that same awe and admiration I felt when I was 19.

When he came out he slowly walked out on stage without face paint or tassels, or his long hair flowing behind him. He was just the man once known as Jim Hellwig who was very tastefully attired in a grey suit and red tie. Warrior walked to his mark on the stage, raised his arms in the air, and the crowd went wild!

While it was certainly an emotional moment, I have to admit I was a little disappointed. I mean, I wanted to see **the Ultimate Warrior**. I wanted the entrance that always sent shockwaves through my entire body. I wanted to see him shake the ropes, pound his chest one more time, and do the press slam motion. Nonetheless, I was happy to see him being immortalized with the other HOF legends.

The next night on WWE's Monday Night Raw I finally got what I wanted. The music hit and I got **that** feeling again! Once again Warrior came out and started walking toward the ring with purpose.

At the end of the entranceway, he grabbed a brown duster that had an airbrushed painting of him on the back, similar to the ring coats he wore later in his career. He put it on, entered the ring, walked over to the hard cam side and...**shook the ropes**!

Memories came flooding back of every match I had ever seen live or on television. Every emotion I'd had and every cheer hit me square in the chest. Nothing else in the world mattered at that moment because I was in Warrior's world, and I was seeing him in all his glory!

After he did some trademark moves, he took the microphone and said words often failed him at times like that. Then he reached into the pocket of the duster, pulled out a Warrior face paint mask and put it on.

4/9/2014, fansided.com

What followed after he shouted, "Shut up, Warriorman, and let me speak!" was the most heartfelt, emotional and humble speech from a man who was infamous for not letting people in. His speech should be used by every motivational speaker, posted in every classroom, and taught to every child by their parents:

"No WWE talent becomes a legend on their own. Every man's heart one day beats its final beat. His lungs breathe their final breath. And if what that man did in his life makes the blood pulse through the body of others and makes them believe deeper in something larger than life then his essence, his spirit, will be immortalized. By the storytellers, by the loyalty, by the memory of those who honor him and make the running the man did live forever.

You, you, you, you, you, *you* are the legend makers of Ultimate Warrior. In the back I see many potential legends. Some of them with warrior spirits. And you will do the same for them.

You will decide if they live with the passion and intensity. So much so that you will tell your stories and you will make them legends, as well. I am The Ultimate Warrior. You are the Ultimate Warrior fans and the spirit of Ultimate Warrior will run forever."

Many consider this to be his farewell address, because there's speculation he felt he was going to die. Reports indicated that Warrior was in good spirits over the weekend, but appeared to be physically uncomfortable or in pain and sweating a lot during his speech.

No one will ever know what really happened. I can, however, say that fans and members of the pro wrestling fraternity lost an Ultimate Brother who got to make peace with those he was at odds with and had an opportunity to say goodbye to.

Maybe making peace was his last mission and his work was done here on earth. Maybe like Julius Caesar, there were no worlds left to conquer.

****

There's not a lot I can say about Warrior that hasn't already been said. I just know that somewhere St. Peter is trying to repair the Pearly Gates after they were blown off their hinges by a crazy guy with long hair and tassels creating chaos in the peaceable kingdom.

Sadly, I never got to meet Warrior face-to-face (I'm sure I will one day, but I can wait until then). All I can say is God bless Jim Hellwig Warrior, Dana Warrior and their children.

Thank you Warrior for being who you were, even if we didn't get it sometimes. You made us feel hope, belief and faith in a higher power and destiny. I dedicate this book to your memory, which will live on forever!

Mission accomplished. Now you can rest in peace......

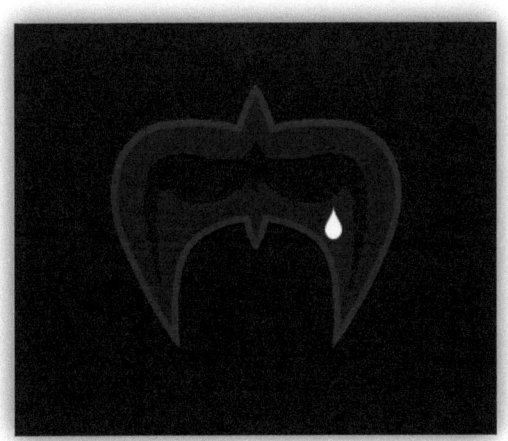

"Every man's heart one day beats its final beat, his lungs breathe their final breath, and if what that man did in his life makes the blood pulse through the body of others and makes them believe deeper in something larger than life, then his essence, his spirit, will be immortalized." ~ Warrior (1959-2014)

ACKNOWLEDGEMENTS

First, I want to thank the world of Professional Wrestling for the thousands of hours of entertainment and enjoyment it has given me.

Second, there are a few specific individuals I want to thank for their contributions to this book (whether they knew they did or not):

Dan Cullen for being my brother, my friend, my tag team partner (he always turned on me -- bastard), and for introducing me to the crazy world of wrestling. This is all his fault.

Ken Wilson for initially training me as a manager.

Delbert Fulmer and **Tiger Conway, Jr.**, for giving me my first shot in Texas.

Booker Huffman and **Tony Norris** for not killing me in the ring.

"Exotic" Adrian Street for his expertise, his no-nonsense training style, and for being a valuable resource.

Kevin Ballew and the gang at Main Event Championship Wrestling in Ohio. Wish I could have done more for all of you.

Lawrence Tyler for giving me the real truth. L.T., I'm grateful for your words of wisdom and support, and I never questioned the truth when it came from you.

Joe Graves; **Pete "The Heat" Petroselli**; **Super Rich**; **Hawaiian Lion**; **R-3**; **"Miracle" Mike James**; **Alexander Hammerstone**; **Toom E. Guci**; **Shot Saxon**; **Dan Draven**; and everyone involved with the former CWFA, now known as Honor Pro. I love you guys, and I'm grateful to be working beside you all.

Joe Vernola, **Mosh Pit Mike**, **and Ray Basura** -- just because you kept me "safe" from cherries and wheat.

Anyone I didn't list, please know that I'm very grateful for all your support.

CONTENTS

Dedication

Acknowledgements

Introduction

Chapter 1: So, You Want to Be a Wrestler?

    If You're a Non-Athlete
    If You're an Athlete
    Mental Exercise and Visualization
    Stay Away From Naysayers!
    Stay True to Yourself
    Be Firm About Your Decision
    Wrestling Will Become Your Life

Chapter 2: Education Equals Knowledge Plus a Few Bumps Along the Way

    My Educational Journey
    Knowledge at Your Fingertips
    Once You Get In
    When Reality Sets In
    Become Acclimated to Your New Community

Chapter 3: KYMS – Keep Your Mouth Shut

That's What Trainers Are For
Illustrating a Point
Treat Others As You Want to Be Treated

Chapter 4: Creating Your Character (aka: Your Gimmick)

Walk the Walk, and Look Like How You Talk
Your Gimmick
Your Character's Name
Mastering Your Character's Promo
Your Character's Gear

Chapter 5: Hitting the Road

Getting to the Promotion
Be Respectful
Don't Even Think About It!
Travel Solo or Carpooling
How Do You Like Your Ribs?
The Venue
Personal Hygiene

Chapter 6: Act Like a Professional

Dress Professionally
Every Job is Important
Play Nice With Others
Do Your Due Diligence
No Job is Too Small

Chapter 7: The Big Wrap-Up

Getting In and Staying In the Industry Are Two Different Things
Competing for Promotion Sports
Drugs, Alcohol and the Ruination of Careers

Chapter 7: Myths Exposed!
1. Since wrestling is "fake" you don't really get hurt.
2. Pro wrestling is like any other job where you get paid and get benefits.
3. Once you become fully trained and start doing road shows, you'll be rich!

Conclusion

Glossary of Terms

Resources

About the Author

INTRODUCTION

Photo Credit Euphoric Moments Photography

Jeff "The Ref" Coles

"We spend 8 hours a day, for 10 months a year, for nearly 17 years sending our kids to school to prepare them for life. In all of that time there is never a course in overcoming adversity, goal setting, sacrifice, perseverance, teammates, or family. I guess that's what wrestling is for.' ~John A. Passaro

Surviving the Ring is based on my many years of experience in professional wrestling. I've outlined the steps you should consider taking if you're serious about a career in this industry. Plus, I'll be covering tips, tools and techniques I learned, as well as things I wish I would have known when I started out in the late 1980s.

First, allow me to give you a little bit of my personal history so you can better understand better why I write this book. I've been a wrestling fan since 1985 when I saw my first full match with Iron Mike Sharp versus Tito Santana. As my friend and I watched Tito put Sharp away with a figure-four leg lock, I said, "Oh, that doesn't hurt."

My friend said, "What?" I said, "There's no way that that hurts." Giving me a sly grin he said, "Get on the floor."

Just as I got down on the floor, my friend quickly put the figure-four leg lock on me (I remembered why they say "never try this at home"). I was hoping to God my knee didn't break because it was hurting like crazy. But at that very moment I was sold on the idea of wrestling, and knew what I wanted for a career.

As a young kid I was interested in superheroes (not necessarily comic books), so it seemed like pro-wrestlers were the closest thing to superheroes I could find. Think about it: They show up at an arena with different names and different attire, then go into the locker room and put on their "costumes." Next they go into the ring and perform seemingly superhuman feats of strength, ability and acrobatics -- good versus evil in its most primal form.

Having rid the city of evil for that night they go back into the locker room, shower, put on "civilian" clothes, and head back out into the real world. Yep, just like a superhero would do.

What I didn't know was the amount of preparation, hard work, dedication and determination that's required to get in and stay in pro wrestling. When you're just starting out is when you need the most advice and help. Back in 1991, it was like being in the middle of an ocean in a boat without oars. I knew where I wanted to go, but had no idea how to get there.

There wasn't the Internet to help me search for schools, promotions, or wrestling gear. It was a very closed industry at that time, which meant no one was under any obligation to help me with my training, get signed on with a promotion, find a pair wrestling boots, give advice on my career, or help me progress in the industry.

Even though it's been almost 22 years since I started in professional wrestling, I haven't been in the industry the entire time. I've always been a fan, and have gotten involved in regional indy promotions from time to time. Officially I've held different positions such as a wrestler, manager, ring announcer, color commentator, and referee. Unofficially I've done things on the "creative" side such as helping with angles, character development, and even theme music selection for some wrestlers. But no matter what I've done, it's a constant education.

As I mentioned, this book is based on my experiences. What I've learned to do and not do will benefit a hopeful wrestler who has no idea where to begin. Things I wish I would have known when I first started out, things I've learned during my career, and things that now seem obvious but didn't make sense until I became more experienced.

****

I'd like to take this opportunity to tell you I'm not going to expose the pro wrestling industry, nor will I reveal any of it secrets. I'm sure many fans read the IWC (Internet Wrestling Community) websites, and are familiar with some industry terms, so I don't feel like I'm violating any secrets by using them.

If you should be fortunate to get accepted to a pro wrestling training school you'll learn these and more, so you'll be ahead of the game by reading my book.

I'll be talking about what you should do to prepare your mind and your body if you're serious about a career in professional wrestling or "sports entertainment." I'll also be talking about some things most people don't consider before they become involved.

Please keep in mind that this isn't a "pro wrestling bible" that should be followed to the letter. It's just a guide written by a guy who had no help when he started, and by writing about his experiences is seeking to help people who want to be wrestlers avoid the same pitfalls, frustrations and disappointments he suffered.

Thanks much, and let's get on with it!

Jeff "The Ref" Coles

CHAPTER 1: SO, YOU WANT TO BE A WRESTLER?

Those seven profound words have been heard by every prospective student at every wrestling school since the inception of pro wrestling. Granted, a lot has changed since the 60s through the 80s when wrestlers were protective about the industry, and would beat up students to prevent them from coming back.

There's the story of legendary Japanese trainer, Hiro Matsuda, and a rather large platinum blond young man who was referred to him by the renowned Brisco brothers for training: Terry Bollea (aka: Hulk Hogan). Matsuda's first question to him was, "So you want to be a wrestler. Huh, kid?" The story goes that Matsuda broke Terry's leg in training on purpose just to see if he had the guts to return after it healed. Once his leg healed, Terry was back at the Matsuda dojo to continue his training.

Photo Credit Jeff "The Ref" Coles

Hulk Hogan, his daughter Brooke and me in 2012. Whoever said we shouldn't meet our heroes was full of crap. I waited 27 years to meet my hero, and it was well worth it because dreams do come true!

(Having met Matsuda in 1977, Bollea was given the last name Hogan by WWWF's Vincent McMahon, Sr. to make him seem Irish and the announcer said he was bigger than the Marvel comic book character, The Hulk.)

When you finally make the decision that you want to be a pro wrestler, the easy part is over and the hard part begins. Many people think they can make the decision to become a pro wrestler, plunk down $2,000 to $5,000 for training and they're in -- which couldn't be further from the truth.

If You're a Non-Athlete

Promotional entertainment venues like WWE (World Wrestling Entertainment), TNA (Total Nonstop Action), Ring of Honor (an American professional wrestling promotion) want extremely physically fit wrestlers.

Pro wrestling is a **very** grueling industry, so if you're not in shape your career won't last (and most likely won't even start). You're going to have to exercise regularly, join a gym, get a personal trainer, and eliminate junk food.

Building Lower Body Strength

Here's an example: Before a tryout with a promotion, one of the promoters invited me to join the warm-up with the training class. Did I say warm-up? Sorry, I meant the complete destruction of my legs with 600 squats, 300 lunges with each leg, and running.

Oh, my God, *the running*! Let's just say that by the time the warm-up was complete, my legs refused to cooperate during the tryout. I ended up looking like crap, which in turn made my opponent look like crap. Needless to say I wasn't invited to be part of the roster, and this proved I wasn't in as good of shape as I thought.

This is why it's of the utmost importance that you exercise your lower body the most. Think about it: During a body slam your legs have to support your weight as well as your opponent's, and if it's happening in the middle or towards the end of a 15 to 20-minute match, you're going to need your legs to be as strong as they were when you first entered the ring.

Squats and lunges are an inexpensive way to increase your leg strength, and you can do them just about anywhere. If you haven't done them before, start out simple with a small number like 50 or 60 during one session. After a week increase the number to 100 or 120, then the following week increase them 200. The longer you keep at it, the stronger your legs will become.

Cardiovascular Conditioning

You'd be surprised at how easy it is to get "gassed" (spending all your energy) within the first five minutes of a match. If you want to be at the main event level, you should be able to work a 60-minute match without getting too gassed.

For instance, if you watch an old Ric Flair (Richard Morgan Fliehr, born February 25, 1949) match that lasted 60 minutes, you'll notice the wrestlers aren't in constant movement. They use rest holds, double downs, and going to the outside.

Each of these tricks helps you to rest a bit during the match. However, you have to be able to look like you can go another 60 minutes after the first 60, so I can't emphasize doing **CARDIO** enough!

The problem I have with running or jogging is the damage it can do to your ankles, knees, and hips. It's fine if you're already running or jogging, but be aware of the impact it can have on your lower body.

Instead, I'd recommend an elliptical machine or an exercise bike where you can get a great cardio workout without much impact to your ankles, knees, and hips. You need to take care of your legs and hips as best you can as you'll be using them a lot.

Eat Healthy

Some people think that since they're working out and getting in shape they can eat whatever they want. That's true to a point, but if you're just starting out you need to switch to eating nutritious meals containing high protein (lots of chicken and fish), green vegetables, lots of fruit, and low-fat, complex carbs, no sugar processed foods. I realize many people have certain dietary restrictions, so you need to create a menu that works best for you.

What's going to get you to the big show faster? Eating McDonald's every day, or having a workout and a nutritional plan to follow? Trainers and promoters look for wrestlers who know how to keep themselves fit and healthy.

So pizza, fried chicken, fast food burgers and junk food should be avoided, but give yourself one day a month to enjoy "cheat meals" where you can eat anything you want and not be nagged about it. But make sure it is **only one day per month**.

If You're An Athlete:

If you're an athlete and have played some sort of high school or college sport, you're already in a better position than the non-athlete. You know how to work out and how to eat right. And if you're involved in a team sport, you know how get along with different types of personalities which is a very important asset to have.

For example, not everyone in the WWE locker room are the best of friends, but they put aside their differences and do what's best for their business or their show. You have to be professional, and learn to work well with difficult people because it's your job.

WWE tends to look more at athletes or wrestlers with some experience under their belt for just these reasons. They're athletic and take their physicality seriously, they're coachable and will listen, and they have experience in dealing with different personalities on a team. It's easier for WWE to train this type of wrestler than it is for them to train non-athletes, because athletes already know what's expected of them.

Mental Exercise and Visualization

Mental exercise is just as important for both non-athletes and athletes. By "mental exercise" I mean you must be able to be in a positive mental state at all times.

Many successful athletes, including Olympic gold medalists, engage in what's called "visualization" -- a method of meditation that consists of sitting in a quiet room in a comfortable chair with their eyes closed and allowing their imagination to create their career path.

The idea is to try to make the image as realistic as possible. For instance, if you're visualizing a match you'll be having during your training class, imagine you and your opponent in the ring. Do you both go for a lock-up? Or do they knee you in the stomach to gain an early advantage?

During this process, visualizing a training wrestling match with an opponent is better than the reality of being in the ring. Why? Because your mind will lay out the blueprint of that match and you can see the end results, which is why many athletes who use visualization are so successful.

Some have even reported a reduction in stress and fear, and had increased confidence in their ability to win the event.

Your mind is the most powerful asset you have, as it has the ability to crush or fulfill your dreams based on what you believe about yourself. This is why it's important to stay positive, keep believing you'll get there, and continue working towards your goal.

Stay Away From Naysayers!

Most importantly, don't let anyone tell you that you're wrong in pursuing your passion, which brings me to another important rule of thumb: Don't look for support or approval from friends or family.

Now, why would I say that? Aren't they supposed to support you in all the decisions you make? Aren't you supposed to be able to trust them to get behind you in your career choice? Well, not exactly and not always.

The funny thing about human nature is that when people are presented with an option or a decision, they typically ask others for their opinion. But by doing that, it opens the door for people to inflict their morals, ethics, objections, and fears on their loved one. For some reason, they feel they have the right to be brutally honest, no matter how much it bursts the person's bubble. "If you didn't want an honest answer, you shouldn't have asked!"

Of course we all want the support of our friends and family for everything we do. Because we love and respect them, their opinion matters. But why would you ask anyone what they think about what you want to do for a career? What is it you're needing from them? Are you looking for approval or support? Are you checking with them to make sure it's okay that you continue on this path?

If you tell your friends and family about your intention to become a professional wrestler, what do you really expect them to say? I guarantee that every single one of them will try to talk you out of it, and get you refocused on another line of work.

They'll probably give you the "odds are" speech. You know the one where you could get hurt or killed, you don't make much money in wrestling, and for every one person who makes it there are thousands who don't.

My question to them would be, "How would you know?" Do you honestly believe a lawyer, accountant, a school teacher or a police officer can provide intelligent, practical answers about the pro wrestling industry? The truth is they can't, and no matter how well-meaning your friends and family are, none of them are ultimately responsible for you or your career. You and only you can make that decision.

To be completely honest, none of my friends or family wanted to see me get involved in pro wrestling. My parents wanted me to be a lawyer or a doctor, and use my brain instead of my body to make a living.

However, what I've learned over the years reinforced that I'm a very creative person, and sitting behind a desk for eight hours a day while allowing "the suits" to dictate my monetary worth just isn't for me. (You're probably very much the same way; otherwise, you wouldn't be reading this book.)

Stay True to Yourself

Allow me to be your support system for a moment. I would say stay true to what you believe about yourself and your ability to create a career in pro wrestling. If you follow these instructions, become healthy and strong, and keep a positive mental attitude, you CAN make it.

What you do with your life is ultimately your choice, so limit whose opinions you ask. People will always toss negative comments about what you're doing in your direction, but you get to decide what you internalize and what you reject.

You can love your friends and family, but don't allow them to talk you out of what you want to do. Like everything in life, you are the master of your own fate.

Be Firm About Your Decision

Along the lines of what I've just discussed about friends and family interjecting their opinions about your career choice, I feel it's incumbent upon me to give you this piece of advice: Make sure this is absolutely what you want to do, because you'll be trading your life for it!

The days of partying with your friends every night, or doing whatever you want whenever you want will be over. They'll be replaced with sensible, nutritional eating habits, and four to five days per week at the gym/training center.

Relationship Survival

That wonderful relationship you currently have could possibly end, even if they love you more than life itself. If they're not supportive of your career choice, they're not going to be supportive when you're on the road leaving them behind for days or weeks on end. Sorry, but the odds are they will cheat on you while you're gone (and possibly vice versa).

If you're a man, your wife or girlfriend is going to demand you don't cheat on them with a "ring rat" while you're on the road (a "ring rat" is similar to rock and roll groupies who hang around after the event looking to hook up with one of the wrestlers). If you're a female wrestler, this same kind of advice applies.

I'd advise against this, mainly because you don't know if you're hooking up with a stalker, or what you'd take home with you. Getting herpes, syphilis, gonorrhea, AIDS – or even having to face an angry husband or boyfriend -- isn't conducive to you having a long career in wrestling, so it's just not worth it.

Now, I know many men and women who have wonderful, supportive relationships because their loved one understands what's required to pursue this kind of dream. Professional wrestling has been known to break up marriages and relationships, but wrestling alone usually isn't the cause for the failure.

It's up to you to explain to your loved one what you expect of them while you continue on your career path. You need to tell them that at some point you'll be going on the road, and may not be home very much while you're getting your career going.

You also need to tell them that you probably aren't going to make enough to live on just from wrestling. They need to be made aware of what you expect from them, and you also need to find out what they expect from you.

Wrestling Will Become Your Life

Honestly, I don't know how much your life will change, but from my own experience I've learned that hardly anything stays the same. You'll miss your friends and your family. You might miss holidays, and important milestones in the lives of your children. But these are the sacrifices that need to be made to get where you want in this industry.

You'll eat, drink and breathe wrestling. You'll think about it while you're awake and while you're asleep, which is the type of passion you need to succeed.

Every day when you wake up you should be thinking, "What can I do today to get me closer to my goal in wrestling?" The short answer is go to the gym. You don't have to kill yourself every day -- maybe you'll alternate toning with bulking.

Plus, you might see other wrestlers you're training with, or someone who can teach you a new way to lift weights. There's always a benefit to going to the gym, and every day you go will make you stronger, healthier, and more knowledgeable.

If you've read my book this far, and you're still intent on becoming a pro wrestler (even though your life will never be what it once was), we can get into the second most important decision you'll make regarding pro wrestling: choosing where to train.

CHAPTER 2: EDUCATION EQUALS KNOWLEDGE PLUS A FEW BUMPS ALONG THE WAY

My Educational Journey

Back in the mid-1980s, after I had made the decision I wanted to be a pro wrestler, I was stuck trying to find a good school. The Internet didn't exist at that time, so I couldn't Google wrestling schools and had to research different schools through other means.

I was aware of several training schools, but wasn't sure if they were still in business. I knew about the Hart Dungeon in Calgary, Canada, but didn't know if it was still active. Plus, I had no idea how long it would take me to drive from Ohio to Canada, or how much it would cost (not just for the school but to also live there).

I knew about Sully's Boxing Gym in Toronto where Adam "Edge" Copeland and Jason "Christian" Reso had trained. I had seen it firsthand in 1988 when my high school concert choir performed in an international choir competition in Toronto. As a bunch of us walked by the gym I looked through the window and saw a wrestling ring, and thought *Wow! This is where I want to train!* I felt that if I moved to Toronto and signed up with Sully's, my home in America would only be six hours away by car.

However, I wasn't aware of all the ramifications of an American living in Toronto going to a wrestling school. Would I need an endorsement from Sully's? Would I have to get a green card? How much would it cost? Even though I probably would have had a better shot at maintaining a wrestling career had I been trained at Sully's, there were too many unknowns I couldn't get answers to. So I decided to stay in the States and find training here.

After I gave up on the notion of training at Sully's, I decided to attend Bill Watts' UWF (Universal Wrestling Federation) training center. This made sense since I wanted to live in Dallas, and I figured that after I completed my training and started wrestling I could set up residence in Texas. Unfortunately, Bill sold his organization to Jim Crockett Promotions and merged it with the NWA before I turned 18, so that flew right out the window.

I was also aware of Killer Kowalski's school in Massachusetts, and Larry Sharp's Monster Factory in New Jersey. However, I was wary of these places because I knew their reputations inside the ring. As a fan trying to get into wrestling, I figured they'd probably kill me.

Since I was a teenager and was pretty ignorant about life outside my hometown, I didn't know if these two schools were going to go by the time-honored tradition of taking a student's money and kicking the crap out of them until they didn't come back. I was serious about my desire to become a pro wrestler, so no one or nothing was going to sway me from my goal. Quite frankly, I didn't have the money to waste, so I knew I had to make a very wise decision.

Knowledge at Your Fingertips

Luckily, people today have the Internet to search for reputable schools with good trainers. Even though finding graduates who've had long-lasting careers in wrestling is a heckuva lot easier now than it was back in the 1980s, you still need to do your due diligence and gather as much research as possible.

Telling you that 90% of a training school's graduates have gone on to WWE, TNA or ROH -- and showing you a website full of pictures of the school and training sessions – won't mean much to you. Of course you'll get a basic idea of what they offer, but you really need to look at the graduates' track records after leaving school.

Just because a school has a long list of graduates who have had careers in wrestling **doesn't guarantee** you'll be one of them. Every school will tell you they can get you to where you want in this industry, but ultimately it's up to you to put in the work, lift the weights, take the bumps and to be coachable and follow instructions.

Training schools give you the key to open the door to the world of wrestling, but you have to put the key in the lock to open the door. If you show up at every session willing to listen and take direction, and apply what you've learned, trainers will help you get to where you want to go. Being a successful graduate brings attention to the school, which brings in more trainees.

Once You Get In

If you do everything like you're supposed to do, your work will speak for itself. Bookers and promoters can usually spot who came from what school as every training program has its own style and brand. So you want to make sure you honor your trainers by learning all they have to teach and applying it to how you work in the ring.

Successful graduates are only one of the many things you should be looking for when investigating a pro wrestling school. Even though this sounds like it should be a given, I'd say the most important thing needed at a training school would be an actual wrestling ring. Not a ring-shaped pile of mats in the corner of a backyard shack -- an actual 16x16' or 18x18' wrestling ring (WWE uses a 20x20' ring).

Some rings are the old-fashioned kind with a giant spring under the middle with cables that cross underneath to keep the ring square. And some are the newer HighSpot rings (available at highspots.com).

It's of the utmost importance that your school have a working, functioning wrestling ring (you'd be surprised at how many don't). The reasoning being that two of the most important things in wrestling happen in the ring: taking bumps and running the ropes.

Bumping is a very important part of the business, and doing it improperly can cause moderate to severe injuries. So it's best to learn the proper way to take a back bump, a running back bump, a face bump, etc.

Learning how to run the ropes properly is another reason why you need to be in good cardiovascular shape and have strong legs. You might watch someone run the ropes on television and think it looks easy, but you'd be wrong because the running is the only easy part. Although they're called "ropes," they're really taut cables wrapped with colorful tape. When you hit the ropes you'll probably get a bruise on your side, which of course will hurt. It's normal and happens to everybody. After a few training sessions, the better you get at running the ropes you won't feel your side hit them, as it'll become a routine part of being in the ring.

When Reality Sets In

After reading this far many of you have probably thought, I'll just go to the WWE Performance Center. I'm going to work for them one day anyway, so I might as well learn their way from the start.

Sorry, but you need to get that out of your mind right now!

As I stated before, WWE is looking for athletes or wrestlers who already have a few years of experience under their belt. If you don't have an athletic, strong body, they won't waste their time on you. They can tell the ones who should be there because they look like they want to be there.

When WWE looks for athletes to bring into their company, they usually look for college football players, wrestlers, and maybe some track and field competitors because they've been coached, keep themselves healthy and in shape, have been in team situations, and because they know they can bring financial value to their company.

I'd advise that if you're a beginner, don't look at WWE as your first option as it may not be the thrilling experience you expect. You're much better off getting your training from an independent wrestling school, mainly because you're going to learn the basics of pro wrestling and not just moves and bumps.

You'll learn wrestler dialect, how to cut a promo, how to create your own character or alter ego, and the basic steps WWE can build on once you get there. But for now, learn all you can from the training school you join. If WWE comes knocking in a couple years and wants to sign you to a contract, they'll teach you how they want you to wrestle while you work for them.

Along the lines of deciding which school you'd like to attend (providing they'll accept you), I'm going to throw in a word that makes everybody cringe: **Budget**! You may be thinking, *All I need is money for the school, and enough gas to get there."* Really? That's all? Where are you going to live? How are you going to eat? What if you need new workout/training clothes?

Maybe the trainer will want you and a few other guys to see a show in another state and you're driving. How will you pay for the gas? You're going to be a sweaty mess after every training session, so how will you pay for laundry? You haven't even begun to get into the cost of your character's costuming as that usually comes out of your pocket. Now can you see why I bring this up?

Let's say you plan on going to an out-of-state training school. Unless you've saved about $10,000 just to start, you might have to get a job while you're training. If that's the case, try to find one that offers a flexible schedule for evenings and weekends as you'll need them free for training and possibly going to shows.

Most wrestling schools don't have a dormitory, but many have partnerships with local hotels. Depending on the school, you may be able to get a good room rate as a student. A one-bedroom apartment or a loft near the school may be your best bet if you can afford it. Make sure the rent includes utilities, as it's better to pay everything in your total rent than paying rent plus electric plus water.

It's also important that your residence has some form of WiFi access. Sometimes the only way you'll have to talk to friends and family is through Facebook or Skype (especially if you can't afford phone bills), so a free WiFi connection is very important to have (you can also check out local coffee houses or WiFi cafes in your area).

Become Acclimated to Your New Community

You've enrolled in the school, paid the tuition and established a residence. Next you should familiarize yourself with the town. Locate a grocery store, laundromat (if your hotel or apartment complex doesn't offer a washer and dryer), a branch of your bank, a mall or shopping center for any incidentals, and a post office. Also, try to find a good restaurant within walking distance. This way you can burn calories going there, and burn off the meal as you walk home. Plus, it's a great way to save on gas.

I'd like to interject that when investigating schools, try to find one affiliated with a wrestling promotion. There many schools that have their own promotions, which is great because you won't have to worry about going out and looking for work. You'll be able to get ring time with people you're familiar with and trust. It will also you get over the initial stage fright of being in the ring in front of people while in a safe environment.

You'll find that the more in-school matches you work, the more comfortable you'll be performing in front of people. As you become more experienced in the ring, going on the road to work a different promotion's show won't seem as frightening. You'll get the best of both worlds because you get to be trained in pro wrestling, and you'll get to work matches with the people you've trained with (which is a plus because you know how each other works).

(I've included some of the more well-known schools with the track records of successful graduates in the Resource section. This list isn't all-encompassing, and I don't endorse most of them because I've never been through their training. I'm merely supplying you with information for you to make your own well-informed decision, but the research is ultimately up to you.)

CHAPTER 3: KYMS - KEEP YOUR MOUTH SHUT

In this chapter I'm going to talk about how a new student should act at the training school. Rest assured, there's a reason for my harsh tone as you need to heed my words and internalize them (especially if you're serious about a career in pro wrestling). Regardless of what you learn in the other chapters, this information will make or break your career. Trust me, I know from experience.

Like I said, you've paid your tuition, found a place to live, and filled the refrigerator to prevent over-spending on fast food or restaurants. You've located all the important places in town, and now you're ready for your first day of training.

You go to the school in your shorts, t-shirt, and sneakers or wrestling shoes, and introduce yourself to everyone since this is your first day. But when the trainer enters and takes center stage **you say nothing. I mean, absolutely nothing**! You stand or sit, keep your mouth shut, and listen to every single word they say.

That's What Trainers Are For

I know what it's like to be in a training school on the first day. You're excited and want to talk about wrestling and spout your knowledge to everyone who will listen. Guess what? Nobody cares that you were in the front row for the 1999 Royal Rumble. Nobody cares that you once drove the Rock's car as a valet. Nobody cares that you got Triple H's autograph at the airport. Seriously, nobody frickin' cares!

Just like every other student at the school, you are **not** there to learn and to figure out who the most knowledgeable wrestling fan is within that room. The trainers won't be impressed with your knowledge because it's "fan" knowledge and has nothing to do with being in an actual ring. You may have seen 15,000 matches, but this doesn't mean you know how to put a match together, how to do the maneuvers, or the whole psychology of the sport.

Trainers are there for a reason. They've been in the industry for a long time and have already been through what you're about to go through, so logically they know more than you. It's their job to teach you, just as it's your job to correctly apply what you learn from them.

During the course of your training an instructor may be giving information to another student who's having some difficulties. Before you jump in with words of wisdom, you need to remember that **it's not up to you to help** because you're not the trainer. That's their job, and over-stepping boundaries can create friction between you, the other student and the trainer.

In situations like this remember **KYMS (keep your mouth shut!**) You'll probably want to prove you've been listening to the trainers and applying what you've learned so you can show everyone you're doing your best. But please don't! You'll be speaking out of turn, and most trainers don't like that at all as it's disrespectful and offensive. Simply put, if you could you'd be teaching the class, but you're not. You're the student and you're learning at this stage. As you continue your training there will be time to ask questions, so you need to save them for more appropriate moments.

I guess the best way to describe how you should view your instructor is they're part Japanese sensei (the master), and part Marine drill instructor. Their purpose is to kick your ass and make you understand why you're getting your ass kicked. They've already done their "time" in wrestling and want to pass their knowledge on to you.

Illustrating a Point

I have a story that quickly illustrates the point. When I was getting back into wrestling a few years ago, I was in a session with a couple guys who had been training for a few months -- one in particular as long as seven to eight months. He was a bodybuilder who also had a good mind for the business and could stay very focused.

But he couldn't cut a promo to save his life, and nobody could figure out why he was having so much trouble. I mean, looking at him you'd wonder why he even needed to talk as his physique spoke for itself. But in this business, how you talk is just as important as how you work.

While the trainers were trying to help him get better with his promo, I tried to help as well since I had already done some acting on camera. I thought I'd share what I had learned about using real emotion when delivering a promo.

I said, "How does your character feel about what's happening?" immediately after which I felt stares burning a hole through my skull. Both the trainer and the promoter were glaring at me, and in that moment I knew I had stepped in it.

When the promoter said, "Um, Jeff...." I knew I had gone too far. So I responded with, "Keep my mouth shut?" He said, "Please do." "Yes, sir. I apologize."

Keep in mind that this was only my second day of being at this school, and I felt like I ended my career again because I was over-eager and was trying too hard to impress them. Probably the worst thing of all was not allowing the trainer do his job, or worse -- thinking I knew more than him. I realized I had insulted him without meaning to, so later that night I apologized to him. I let him know I was just trying to help, and that if he had wanted my help he would have asked for it.

This is a lesson to the know-it-all's who think they're going to go to a training school, drop a little bit of fan knowledge, and expect everyone to fall at their feet and call them the "master of pro wrestling." I can tell you unequivocally that **it won't happen.** So don't waste your time or energy, don't shoot yourself in the foot, and don't end your career before it starts.

You'll have to admit that while you may be a big fan of the industry, you know little to nothing about what goes on in pro wrestling. So allow your mind to become a blank slate, and let the trainers scribble information across that big whiteboard in your brain. Pay attention to what they're doing and why they do it a certain way. Showing your trainers respect, courtesy, and giving your all will carry you a long way from student to professional.

Treat Others As You Want to Be Treated

I also want to mention something about how you should treat the other trainees or students. If you come into a class that's been running for while, you'll be the low man on the totem pole which is where you don't want to stay. So you need to check with the trainers to find out when a new class is scheduled to start. It's much better to come in fresh at the beginning than midway through an ongoing class where everyone is ahead of the game.

Your classmates are there for the same reason you are: They're there to apply what they learn, and become professional wrestlers. As I mentioned before you may not like everybody in your class, but you do have to learn to work with them.

I've seen guys who didn't like each other and didn't want work together put their differences aside and put on an incredible match for the fans. They understood that the point of the business is to entertain, and not to kill anyone or get killed. During an actual match you're literally putting your life into their hands and they are putting their life into yours, so you never want to enter a ring with bad feelings or a grudge.

There are wrestlers who will put having a problem with another wrestler on Twitter or Facebook. Their fans become emotionally involved, and it becomes an unnecessary (and unprofessional) mess. If for some reason you have a problem with one of your classmates, do yourself a favor and try to work out the problem with them. If you take the problem to the promoter or the trainer you run the risk of being called a whining, cry baby (which is similar to telling the teacher on another student in grade school).

You don't want to be known as a tattletale or a whistle blower; you want to be known as someone who will work problems out in a fair and amicable way. If you and that person can't resolve the issue, you may need to take it to the promoter or the trainer. But you should make an attempt to solve the problem first before you go that route.

I'm not going to say the wrestling industry is perfect and that nobody fights with each other, because that's just not true. But the professionals will do their best to "squash all beef" with students or workers who haven't been treating them fairly or in a professional manner.

There are enough problems in life and in professional wrestling, so why add more problems to the list? Become a problem solver and a locker room leader. Whatever you do don't allow it to get physical because nobody wins.

Both of you could find yourselves kicked out of the school, out of wrestling, and looking on Monster.com for your next job, and I know you don't want that to happen. So try your best to get along with everyone as much as possible, and be very wise about the steps you take to remedy a negative situation.

CHAPTER 4: CREATING YOUR CHARACTER (AKA: YOUR GIMMICK)

Photo Credit Jeff "The Ref" Coles

The Atomic Punk: This was when I broke in in 1991. I was the Atomic Punk in Houston as part of the Texas All-Pro Wrestling. I think a certain "D-Generate" stole the gimmick. Oh, well...

Everyone who's ever considered becoming a pro wrestler has some kind of character image or "gimmick." (The word "gimmick" has several meanings in wrestling, but for now I'll be using it to refer to your character image.)

Your character is a visual explanation of who you are. You've seen wrestlers who walk out of the back towards the ring, and before they say a word you get an immediate idea of who they are (or at least trying to portray).

Let's imagine for a moment that you're at a show with no prior knowledge of wrestling, and out comes the Undertaker. Do you need to hear him talk to know he's a bad ass? Of course you don't, because you can see who he is in the way he dresses, the way he slowly makes his way to the ring, and all the entrance special effects he uses. You know exactly who he is and what he's about.

Walk the Walk, and Look Like How You Talk

A friend and former trainer of mine, "Exotic" Adrian Street, once told me, "Nobody is going to pay their hard-earned money to see a guy who looks like their neighbor." (Those words have stayed with me throughout the years, which is why I coined it the "neighbor gimmick.") And he was right: People don't want to see wrestlers looking like regular people we see at the grocery store or pumping our gas. They want to see fancy, bright, extravagant, "blinged" costumes.

Photo Credit Jeff "The Ref" Coles

This is from The Islander, a local paper in the Pensacola/Gulf Breeze area of Florida where I trained with "Exotic" Adrian Street (far left).

Unfortunately, there are a lot of wrestlers who do use the "neighbor gimmick," because they show up to wrestle in basically what they wore all day: T-shirt, jeans or cargo shorts, and tennis shoes.

Yes, John Cena wears a t-shirt, cargo shorts and tennis shoes to wrestle. Well, he does now. But before he made it to WWE (and for a little while after he debuted) he wore wrestling trunks and boots. WWE had him go for the rapper gimmick, which is where the tennis shoes and cargo shorts came from. When he dropped that gimmick he kept the same "non-gear" as his wrestling attire, and now everybody thinks it's okay to wrestle in it. So if you don't look like a pro wrestler, you'll never be able to convince anyone you are.

Think about some of the most memorable wrestlers in history like Ric Flair. In the 1970s, most guys were wearing the standard black, green, or red trunks with boots and maybe kneepads. They'd come to the ring in jackets or vests, which was very boring for the fans. Then here comes Ric Flair with his gorgeous ring robes adorned with sequins and feathers.

During this period of time in the industry, seeing a wrestler come out with that kind of opulence draped upon him you couldn't help but feel that he was **the man**. Why? Because he looked like the man regardless of what he did in the ring.

Randy Savage is another wrestler who comes to mind. When he started wearing sequined capes and headbands in WWF in the 1980s, it was much more glamorous than what most fans were used to seeing. When he transitioned to wearing the jacket, shirt, tights and cowboy hat in the late 80s to the mid-90s, I remember tuning into the weekly WWF programming just to see what he was wearing.

Let's go back even further. If you're a fan you may remember "Superstar" Billy Graham, who went against conventionality by wearing tie-dyed tights and t-shirts with a feather boa over his shoulders, and crazy looking sunglasses. After Graham came Jesse "the Body" Ventura, who used Graham's ridiculous sunglasses and feather boa, but also dressed himself outrageously.

Why would they go to these extremes? It wasn't the norm. It was different. It was flashy. It became their gimmick. This goes all the way back to the wrestler, Gorgeous George, in the late 1950s, and later echoed by "Exotic" Adrian Street. The one thing each of these wrestlers had in common was their ring gear, and their gimmicks needed no explanation. All you had to do was look at them and you immediately got who they were.

Your Gimmick

Before we get into gear, let's talk about your gimmick, your alter-ego, your character. In other words, the "other you." Admittedly, you can drive yourself crazy trying to come up with a gimmick. You want to be an original, but it's kind of hard to do when it seems like every persona has been taken, so at this point don't worry about originality. Of course, at some point you're going to have to come up with something that's truly yours, but don't allow yourself to get stuck on finding it at this point.

The thing you need to realize is once you're wrestling on a regular basis, you'll be more "in character" than not, so your gimmick should be comfortable in any situation. If you have an idea for one that sounds good but you're not really sure if it feels right, you'll want to make adjustments along the way.

I've known wrestlers who were shy and introverted in real life, but their gimmick of being a brash loudmouth worked for them. I think the best way to figure out what your character should be is by taking a hard look at the real you and making your character exactly the opposite.

For example, I'm a pretty nice, friendly guy and can be friends with pretty much anybody. However, my character was a trash-talking, hateful, downright mean sonofabitch. I'd scream at old ladies sitting at ringside, and make fun of them and the fat man sitting next to them. I'd call the entire audience a bunch of "nothin' happenin', redneck, white trash, blue collar slobs." They hated me and I loved it. But Jeff Coles wasn't saying those things – my character was, which was how I had the courage to do it. It was all part of the show and wasn't personal to anyone -- it was just me doing what I had to do.

Along these lines, it's important to remember that this "other you" is strictly for the purposes of entertaining your fans, and isn't an excuse to live out your violent fantasies in real life. The only times you should be in character outside of a wrestling show is if you're giving interviews, signing autographs in public, or meeting fans in public.

So don't allow yourself to get caught up in your character as it can consume you. I know from personal experience that staying in character beyond the ring blurs the lines between fantasy and reality. In other words, you'll start to believe that you **are** your character, which is in no way healthy and is a surefire way to get yourself locked up in a sanitarium. Yes, we are performers of fantasy in a real world -- not the other way around -- so don't lose yourself to your gimmick.

Your Character's Name

It seems that within the last 15 years or so every would-be wrestler wanted to be a bad ass in the ring like "Stone Cold" Steve Austin. I hate to break it to you, but you can't be. There was only one Steve Austin, so don't think for one second that coming up with something similar isn't a slap in his face.

I knew a wrestler who went by "Even Colder" -- a Steve Austin look-alike who won a contest at a bar (I'm not sure if he ever have any actual wrestling training other than performing as "Stone Cold Stunner"). I'm not trying to disparage the guy because he did look an awful lot like Austin, but I often wondered how Austin himself felt about it. My point here is you can still be a bad ass, but be original about it.

Here's another personal example: When I was training with Adrian Street and was trying to come up with a character, I told him that everybody in wrestling was trying to be a bad ass and that I wanted to do something different. He told me the same thing I told you earlier: That whatever character I chose had to be something I was comfortable in portraying.

So I thought about characters I liked, and tried to equate one of them to my new persona. I thought I could wear gear with the Looney Tunes characters on it. I'd call myself "The Warner Brother," and use the Looney Tunes music to be my theme music.

Photo Credit Jeff "The Ref" Coles

Okay, go ahead and laugh. Sometimes, it's better to try something new than to be the next so-and-so. Go out on a limb and be the first YOU!

I figured I could create a tag team with one of the many wrestlers using the Doink the Clown gimmick in the indys. I thought kids would love it because of the comedy antics we could pull in the ring, and I'd have a great time doing it. It was a sound idea and I even had the gear made (I still have it), but I wasn't able to bring it to fruition for several reasons. You can find inspiration for a character in the most unlikely of places, so don't limit your creativity.

As I mentioned in my personal story above, I asked Adrian to help me come up with my gimmick. It's always good to ask for advice or direction, but keep in mind this is your character and will belong solely to you, so be very selective in who you ask for advice. Some people may have some great ideas that add value to your character, while others may try to steer you down a road that has absolutely nothing to do with the personality you're envisioning, which is fine because they're brainstorming and trying to help you out.

However, they should understand that even though you're asking for their advice it doesn't mean you're going to take it. This character is your creation, so you need to determine how many "artists" you're going to allow to put brushstrokes on your masterpiece. It probably won't come together all at once, but if you can get a general idea of who your character is, what he's about, why he's in this promotion and where he's going, the additional details will reveal themselves.

While you're refining your character you need to decide how it will talk to people, which will be particularly important during promos (interviews). In this day and age, people tend to focus more on what's being said rather than the way it's said. There was a time when a promo was just a bunch of screaming and hollering at the camera or interviewer with a lot of "Let me tell you something..." and "Brother..." Nowadays, fans really want to hear what the wrestlers have to say.

If you watch Monday Night RAW showcasing CM Punk or Daniel Bryan or even The Shield, you'll notice they don't scream -- they talk. Raising your voice doesn't necessarily raise the intensity of your promo. Screaming "I'm gonna get you, John Cena! I'm going to eat your face!" will definitely get someone's attention. But if you can look straight into the camera and feel the emotion behind what you're about to say, the intensity will be visible in your eyes and your voice. You can be calm and articulate while still being intense.

Chris Jericho mentioned Javier Bardem's character from the movie, "No Country for Old Men." Bardem's character, Anton Chigurh, never yelled or screamed, and never went ballistic about what he was going to do. He spoke very calmly when telling people what he was going to do, and then did it without screaming and yelling.

When Jericho started wearing a suit to the ring for promos, he was utilizing that method of being very calm and understated, while at the same time very direct and intense. So you'll need to decide what you want your character to be. Are they screaming and yelling everything they're going to do to their opponent? Or are they more stoic, and calm but intense? Make sure the promo style fits with your character's gimmick.

Mastering Your Character's Promo

You don't need to be at school to master cutting a promo, as it can be done from your residence or any other location. It's very simple and fun to do because you get to be completely ridiculous when you're in character.

When you first start developing your character's persona, I'd recommend standing in front of the bathroom mirror with a hairbrush to use as a microphone, select any current wrestler you'd would like to cut a promo on, and allow your mind wander for things to say.

The three most important things that should be included in your promo are:
1. Who are you?
2. Why are you here?
3. Where do you go from here?

The first question is pretty obvious as you're going to tell people who you are. You don't have to give a long drawn out explanation or backstory; your name will work just fine.

The second question gets into the meat of your existence in the promotion. Why are you in the promotion? What's the goal you're trying to reach?

The third question is a little more difficult since it's hard to say where you'll go once your main goal has been accomplished. You may have some ideas, but that's left entirely to the booking committee. You can say something like, "After I win the heavyweight title I'm going to find a tag team partner and take the tag titles. Then I'll have all the gold!" Answering these three questions will give you a solid promo.

Also, if it fits your character you should come up with a tagline or catch phrase to use at the end of the promo. If it's well received, you can consider making t-shirts with the slogan on it and sell them at shows for extra money.

If after trying all of the above you're still having trouble with your promo, you may want to talk to the trainer about pairing you with a manager. Managers have been used to help wrestlers who are having troubles with their promos. Managers are mouthpieces – they're hype men. They talk about what their man is going to do to his opponent in the ring. A manager might help your situation until you feel you can confidently take the microphone and deliver better promos.

Your Character's Gear

Okay, you've got your character, your slogan, and you've become pretty good at delivering promos. So now we're going to talk about your gear, which refers to your wrestling outfit and peripherals -- anything you're going to wear to transform you into your wrestling alter ego. Obviously this would be tights or trunks, wrestling boots, knee and elbow pads, wrist tape, forearm sleeves, a hood (mask), a ring jacket or robe, and any accents such as bandanas, gloves, face paint, etc.

Contrary to popular belief, you **do** need to buy the right gear. I don't know how I can make this any more clearly stated: **Gear equals professionalism**. Walmart board shorts or MMA trunks won't cut it. You'll be dressing for matches as a professional wrestler and not like your neighbor.

(If you don't believe that gear is important, check out a Facebook page called Trash Bag Wrestlers that pokes fun at wrestlers who don't wear appropriate gear, or think that gear should be purchased at Walmart.

On that page are Under Armor shirts and shorts, Punisher shirts, pleather board shorts, tennis shoes, blue jeans, skull t-shirts, MMA gloves, and way too many Confederate flags. To be honest if I ran my own promotion I wouldn't hire any of those people -- even if they can work – because they look like they got their gear at a thrift store. You don't want to be someone the world pokes fun at, so **please don't** be one of them!)

There are many retail locations to buy actual wrestling gear, and many wrestlers buy the materials and have someone sew them together. (I've included website links for wrestling gear and boots in the Resources section. I don't personally endorse any of these sources, so this is strictly for your information. But please use them because I don't **ever** want to see you on TBW!)

CHAPTER 5: HITTING THE ROAD

Photo Credit Euphoric Moments Photography

Sergio Vega covers Awesome Andy for the pin. 1...2... OH, HE KICKED OUT!

(The information I'll provide in this chapter may be the same you'll hear from your trainers. But I thought it would be nice to give you a heads up about what goes on when you're finally on the road.)

Obviously, this will be after you've spent a few months training and applying your craft with your school's promotion. Usually, the trainer or the promoter (or both) will give you "the blessing," which means you can work in other promotions that will give you more visibility. And if you do a good job for that promoter, they might recommend you to other promotions, which is how you network in professional wrestling.

NOTE: I don't know if "the blessing" is an actual term used in pro wrestling. I just think it makes sense because your trainer is vouching for you by allowing you to work for another promoter, so I guess I'd consider that being blessed. But just to be safe, you may want to check with your trainer first.

Getting to the Promotion

Now that you've been training for several months, your trainer should give you an idea of what to expect when traveling to another promotion. Chances are they know the promoter and can tell you what type of person they are, how to communicate with them, and give you contact information.

It will be up to you to call the promoter and verify that your trainer has spoken with him about putting you in the next show. It's also up to you to find the location of the event and possibly a motel or hotel nearby, unless the promotion is only a few hours away and you'd rather drive home afterwards. My rule of thumb is any drive longer than six hours one way for a show means I'll be staying overnight and driving back the next day.

You might ask why I'd do that when it's only six hours to get back, so let's look at this example:

- You drove for six hours to get to the event.
- Your adrenaline will be pumping because you're excited to be working in a new area in front of new people.
- By the time the show is over it'll probably be after 10:00 p.m. More often than not people from the show want to get something to eat, so you tag along. By the time you're done, it's after midnight.
- Once the adrenaline stops flowing your body crashes, and all you'll want to do is go to bed.

The old adage "it's better to be safe than sorry" always proves to be true. I'd rather be safe than try to make it back when I don't have to. Hotel or motel rooms may be expensive, but so are lawsuits because you fall asleep behind the wheel and crash into a bus full of kids. I know that's a bit of an exaggeration, but I think you see where

I'm going with this.

I've heard stories of wrestlers driving back after an event where they dozed off several times at the wheel with a full car of guys. When I heard that I told them, "Guys, I'll drive next time even if I'm not on the show as that's just not safe," so now I'm a "snooze" designated driver and that's what I'd recommend for you. Either stay in the same town that night and drive back home the next day, or have a friend who's not working the show be your driver.

I realize that in the indys wrestlers travel from one show to another without getting a chance to stop at home. This will happen as you get your experience level up and start traveling more throughout the country, but it's not something you need to worry about now. However, I still stand by my point of finding someone to drive, or if you're too tired to drive, stay overnight.

Be Respectful

Along the lines of staying in hotels or motels, you need to be respectful and don't trash the room. I've never understood why musicians, athletes or anyone would purposefully destroy property as it proves nothing. You'll end up paying for repairs, and when you're just starting out in wrestling you're not going to make enough to cover your expenses much less a repair bill. Plus news travels fast, and it can ruin your reputation before you even build one.

You need to remember that if you return to that town for a future show, do you think that hotel will allow you to come back? Of course they won't. So be smart and treat the hotel, bar and restaurant staff with respect and friendliness.

Most people think that all wrestlers are tough, mean, and abusive, so surprise them by not "gimmicking" them and be real person. Use good manners such as "Can I please get a wakeup call for 7:00 a.m.? Can you please tell me where the ice machine is? Thank you so much. Thank you for your help. Thank you for the directions, etc., etc." Be a human being, and speak to people the way you want them to speak to you. Trust me, they'll remember you the next time you come to town and will go out of their way to help.

You may not believe I need to tell you these things as they should be logical, but you have a reputation to uphold. So don't take towels, ashtrays, matches or even the hotel stationery as they cost the hotel money. When they have to replace amenities they raise the room rates, so help them keep costs low and don't be a jerk. Bring travel size bottles of shampoo and body wash if you use it, and any other bath items you'll need.

One more note: If you stay in an expensive hotel, be smart with your spending and **avoid the minibar like the plague**! Twenty dollars for a packet of peanuts or a soda isn't a smart financial investment, when for $20 you can have a good meal in an outside restaurant and have money left over.

Don't Even Think About It!

Events held in venues like high school gyms or concert halls usually have a lot of "stuff" lying around in locker rooms or the back stage area. It could be anything from 2x4s, football jerseys, strength training equipment, tools, promotional posters, etc.

Your first thought might be, *Great! A souvenir!* and take it. But don't even think about it, as taking something from a venue, no matter how big or small, is theft pure and simple. Even if you're not getting paid for the show, it doesn't give you the right to try to recoup your losses by taking (stealing) something. Something as inexpensive as pilfering a t-shirt can prevent you, and possibly the whole promotion, from returning to that venue.

When I was wrestling in Texas, our show was held at the local high school. A laundry bin in the locker room was full of dirty clothes the football team had worn for practice. One of the workers took a t-shirt and a pair of shorts to wear to the ring to get the home town fans cheering for their team (which would also get them excited for the wrestlers).

When I saw him taking them I thought, *Great, a souvenir!* and I also took a t-shirt from the bin. One of the other workers came over to me and said, "Why are you trying to steal a shirt? That belongs to the school. Come on, man, we want to be able to come back here."

I thought about it for about 5 seconds, tossed the shirt back into the bin, and said, "Of course you're right -- I didn't think of it that way. Sorry about that."

The guy smiled because he knew he had gotten me to think about what I was doing (and I never forgot what he said). If he hadn't been there to point out my error, I probably wouldn't have realized it until it was too late.

Leave everything as you found it. You want the promoter and the venue owner to think of you and the entire roster in a favorable way. Not taking things is a good way to show your respect and gratitude for being able to have a show at that venue.

Traveling Solo or Carpooling

Traveling solo or carpooling with other wrestlers is totally up to you. Personally I'd recommend carpooling, especially if you're traveling with guys you don't know that well. It's a great way to get to know each other better, make new friends, and best of all accumulate road stories.

Let's face it, wrestlers are weird, and lots of funny stuff happens that fans never hear about. I've heard some hilarious stories and always wished I was there to see them. I won't go into details because it's not my place, but sometimes the only cure for a crappy match is a good story that evolves from it.

How Do You Like Your Ribs?

Along with the road stories be prepared to get "ribbed," which are practical jokes wrestlers play on each other. I've seen some ribs that made me fall on the floor laughing, and I've seen ones that made me want to vomit because they were disgusting.

A good ribbing is one that doesn't cost the victim any money or harm, or conflicts with his morals (but you can still get a good laugh out of it). Wrestlers do this to break the monotony while being on the road and the daily grind of being in wrestling.

Being a neophyte in the industry, you can be guaranteed that the more seasoned wrestler will rib you. I can't tell you what to expect as they're all different (i.e., they may hide your gear bag, or drop a deuce [take a dump] in it).

If you do get ribbed -- I'm sorry, WHEN you get ribbed – you'll have two ways to react. The first is to become angry, upset, embarrassed and ready to seek vengeance. The second is to laugh at the rib and at yourself, and congratulate the guy who did it on a job well done. Which way do you think is best to handle a ribbing? Of course, the answer is the second one if you want to stay in good graces with your fellow wrestlers.

They'll also use ribs to see if you're brave enough to be in this business. If you go crying to the promoter, you're pretty much done. Again, your colleagues won't want to be associated with a tattletale or cry baby, so you'll need to take it in stride.

That being said, this doesn't mean you can't rib them back. When it comes to ribbing give as good as you get, as this is a good way to get respect from the other wrestlers because you didn't break down and cry. You took it like a man (or a woman, whatever gender you are as a wrestler) and gave it back in kind. However, if you're not the kind to take it in stride or don't care to retaliate, tell the wrestler they pulled a good rib on you and buy them a drink after the show.

I've said many times that professional wrestling is its own community, a fraternity, a brotherhood, a fellowship. They're people you'll be spending your entire professional career with, so it's better to have as many friends as you can than people you have problems with. Living in the wrestling world should be fun, and ribbing is just another way wrestlers make things more enjoyable. If you don't take ribbing personally, you'll have a much longer career in pro wrestling.

The Venue

Now I'm going to talk about the venue where the event will be held. In independent wrestling, venues can range from a bingo hall, high school gym, or a retail space in a shopping center. The thing to remember is when you're at a venue you need to treat it with the same respect as you would a hotel. One again, don't trash it and don't steal anything as you want to be able to come back.

I've been at events where guys would urinate or defecate in some corner which is very disrespectful to the person who owns the property, the promoter who's running the show, the other wrestlers on the card, and the fans who can probably smell that nastiness from their seats. If there's no bathroom at the venue, use the back stage door and go outside to pee.

There are many stories about wrestlers who crap their pants while in the ring. Yes, it does happen, but if it happens to you try not to let it happen too often. If you have to go number two and there's no bathroom, either carry a roll of toilet paper with you and find a secluded area out back, or just try to hold it.

Some venues don't have restroom facilities, so try to find out ahead of time from the promoter if there are restroom and/or shower facilities and plan accordingly. If you're not staying at a hotel in town after the show, you may want to take advantage of the shower facilities at the venue, especially if you're about to get into a car with four or five other guys.

Personal Hygiene

Now that I opened the door to body order I'd like to discuss something that should be common sense, but unfortunately there are some people who need to be told that **personal hygiene is very important**.

You need to keep your body, clothes and your gear clean and washed at all times. One of the biggest complaints I hear from wrestlers during training is how so-and-so smells bad, and no one wants to train with them because they stink. Of course you'll end up having body odor after training and an event, but you should smell good the rest of the time.

Even if I was very active during the day -- whether doing yard work, exercising, or anything of a physical nature – I'd always shower and put on clean clothes before training as it was a professional courtesy. You don't want to smell someone else's odors, so don't expect anyone to smell yours. So shower daily -- more than once if necessary – and wash your clothes and your gear.

Emptying a can of AXE body spray into your gear bag and all over yourself won't make you or your gear smell clean; it'll just mask the odor if not make it worse. If you have more than one set of gear, keep the used items away from the clean ones. Have an extra bag big enough to hold your dirty clothes and gear, and keep it in the trunk of your car until you can get to a laundromat. Along those lines, you should always have laundry detergent and a couple rolls of quarters just in case your only option is a Laundromat instead of facilities at a hotel or your apartment.

And for God's sake wash your hair, brush your teeth and use mouthwash as you'll be in close quarters with other wrestlers! Yes, cleanliness is next to godliness, and can prevent you from getting a good beating in the locker room!

CHAPTER 6: ACT LIKE A PROFESSIONAL

Although professional wrestling means you're getting paid to perform in matches, there's more to being a pro wrestler than getting paid for what you do. I learned a lot of these lessons too late, which cost me good positions working with great people. Therefore, I feel it's my duty to pass those lessons on to the champions of tomorrow.

First, let's talk about the way you dress. Most workers at an indy show usually wear t-shirts, jeans or shorts, and tennis shoes. There's nothing wrong with that, but I was taught to dress for the job you want -- not the job you have. In other words, if you want to make it to WWE you have to dress the part. Sure, you could show up to an event in jeans and a t-shirt, but what does kind of image does it give people? It says you don't think you'll ever make it to the big promotions, so why bother.

Dress Professionally

"Clothes make the man [or woman]. Naked people have little or no influence on society." ~Mark Twain

There's nothing wrong with showing up in a clean button-up or polo shirt, khaki or dress slacks, and polished shoes. If you want to earn a million bucks you have to dress like a million bucks. I realized how much sense that made when I first heard it. I used to show up in t-shirts and jeans, but now I look more professional when I arrive at the venue. It does something to your psyche to dress nice, because if you look professional you'll feel professional.

This is just a little piece of advice that you can take or leave. But I guarantee that if you're working a show and scouts are back stage, the better dressed worker is going to get their attention quicker than a bunch of guys in t-shirts and shorts.

Maybe this will help you understand it better: You own a company and are holding interviews to fill a top notch position. It comes down to two candidates who have the same experience and education. One is dressed in a clean, pressed suit, polished shoes, a nice tie, and looks well-kempt. The other interviewee is wearing a wrinkled shirt, its sleeves are rolled up, and it's not tucked into his pants. His khaki pants are stained, and he's wearing work boots.

Who would you hire? Of course most companies would hire the one who's dressed for success. While the other man's abilities, experience and education may qualify him for the position, he doesn't look like a professional. Clothes **do** make the wrestler man [or woman], so if you want to be a professional wrestler you need to dress professionally.

Everyone's Job is Important

I mentioned this before, but it bears repeating since we're talking about professionalism. Everyone from the most seasoned veteran to the camera and audio guys, to the concessionaires, to even the green rookies who just started at the school, **you need to respect everyone** in the venue as they're doing their part to put on the best event possible.

The camera guy isn't any more important than the audio guy, the concessionaire, or the person taking the tickets as everyone has an important role at the venue. As long everyone does their job to the best of their ability, the show will be memorable not only to the fans but to everyone who had a hand in its success.

Play Nice With Others

Photo Credit Euphoric Moments Photography

Johnny Manson covered by Woody Hunter, and me ... counting.

As I said before, there may be some people you don't get along with for whatever reason. Whatever issues you may have towards them or vice versa, you have to diffuse the situation as quickly as possible.

Don't wait for them to come to you because they might not. Chances are you're going to be working with that wrestler in a lot of different areas, so the best thing to do is to solve any personal problems before the show starts, especially you're going to be working with them. Even if you can't completely solve the problem, at least they'll know you tried.

You don't necessarily have to like everyone, but you do have to be professional which includes getting rid of any lingering issues between you and any workers. Wrestling is a tough world to be in, and it'll become a lot tougher if you allow heat to exist between you and other wrestlers.

Let's think about it another way. Maybe during a match the other wrestler does something you aren't prepared for. Or they'll hit you too hard, put a move on you that you hadn't taken before, or kick out of the finish. Whatever it is let it go until after the match is over, then calmly discuss what happened with your opponent back stage. Don't yell obscenities or call them names.

Again, it's all about professionalism. If you worked in an office, you wouldn't walk up and down the halls screaming that so-and-so screwed up a client's account or was a terrible person. Instead you'd take them aside and calmly find out what happened and if it can be fixed. That's being rational and in control of your emotions, and shows that you genuinely want to solve the problem instead of making it worse.

If you're known as someone who tries to solve problems rather than create them, you'll be a welcome addition to any promotion. Please keep in mind this doesn't mean you have to solve everybody's problems since the onus is on them do to it for themselves. But you can give them good advice on how to turn a bad situation into a good one.

Do Your Due Diligence

Part of being a professional wrestler is to be aware of what's going on the night of the venue. Obviously, one of the first things you'll do when you check in is to see the booker who will tell you what's going on with your match.

The next step is to find your opponent for the evening. He may have already talked to the booker, so you'll want to ask him if he knows what the two of you will be doing during the match. Find out what kind of match it will be (i.e., a regular one fall match, steel cage, first blood, or last man standing).

You'll also want to know how long the match is supposed to be. This is very important to know if you're filming for television, since going two minutes short or over can throw the whole schedule off. You'll either cut into someone else's match time, or the production crew has to find two minutes of filler for the viewers. Either way it causes a problem for production. You want everything about the match to go as smoothly as possible, so stick closely to your times.

You'll also want to be aware of everything you can expect to happen in the match. For instance, while you're talking with your opponent find out if anything is going to happen, like a run-in. If either of you have any questions or concerns, talk to the booker together and don't try to figure it out by yourself as you could ruin the entire match (and it's not professional).

No Job is Too Small

You'll always have opportunities to prove your professionalism and desire to maintain a career in this industry, so you should be of the mindset that there's no job too small.

Let's say you're still being trained at the school but are about to be part of your first show, there are plenty of things you can do to help get the show started on time. Primarily if the ring needs to be set up, you should be on hand to help.

Pitching in is part of paying your dues. I did it when I first started in wrestling and managing, and even when I was doing ring announcing, color commentating, and as a referee. While I may not set the ring up anymore, I do help carry the posts, frame and ropes into the venue. As a rookie you'll be expected to carry the pieces of the ring into the venue as well as help set it up, and you'll learn how to tie down the canvas and the ring skirts.

The next step after assembling the ring is setting up the chairs for the fans, which **everybody** should be doing. Now, I realize there may be some workers who have merchandise (t-shirts, 8x10 promo photos, DVDs, etc.) and will be busy setting their table up prior to a show. If that's the case, make sure you have a few chairs at the table so that anyone who will be helping them sell the merchandise have a place to sit.

Incidentally, merchandise (aka: "merch") is also known as a "gimmick." Hearing someone ask "Got any gimmicks?" usually means if you have any merchandise to sell. You probably won't have any as a rookie, but later on in your career it will be a good idea to have merchandise to sell to your fans. It's a great marketing tool to get your name out into the world, and an easy way for you to pad your pockets with extra cash.

By following these tips on professionalism, you can avoid pitfalls many young wrestlers face when they're first getting into the business. I wish I had known a lot of this when I first started, so you're already one leg up on me. How about that!

CHAPTER 7: THE BIG WRAP-UP

Photo Credit Euphoric Moments Photography

Walking to the ring with the Heavyweight championship belt. This was for the final match of our Heavyweight title tournament for CWFA.

I previously stated that much of what you're reading will be taught to you in school (depending, of course, on their instructors and their curriculum). The purpose for writing this book is to prepare you before you go to school so you have a better idea of what it means to be in the world of pro wrestling.

Looking back to when I first made the decision to become a pro wrestler, I wish there were resources like this available. This isn't information for you to spout off to other students; it's to assist you in your training.

Even though most of it is common sense, you'd be surprised at how many people don't think of things like healthy eating, being respectful on the road, and keeping themselves and their gear clean. So just to be thorough, I've included it so people with or without common sense are aware of it.

Getting In and Staying In the Industry Are Two Different Things

After everything you've read about becoming a pro wrestler, this next statement may be confusing: It's easier to **get** into professional wrestling than it is to **stay** in professional wrestling. From personal experience, I learned that just because you get training doesn't mean you're going to be the next John Cena. You'll have to keep at it every day by working out, practicing promos, training, etc. It's all part and parcel of becoming a pro wrestler, and never stops until you retire or quit.

When you perform a move during training and the trainer says, "That sucks," don't take it personally. He didn't say **you** suck, but the way you performed that moved sucked, so don't be hard on yourself. Take this as an opportunity to get better and **don't quit**! Do the move over and over and over, and keep doing it until you get it right and then do it some more. Repetition is the best way to get better as long as you're doing it correctly.

There are thousands of wrestlers in the world, but realistically there's only one style of body slam, only one arm drag, and only one **vertical suplex** (a defensive throw that involves lifting the opponent, and bridging or rolling to slam them on their back).

Photo Credit April Pierson Photography

Pete "The Heat" Petroselli on the receiving end of an Alexander Hammerstone exploder suplex. And brother, when it explodes...it EXPLODES!'

Some wrestlers may put a twist on some of these moves, but it doesn't matter who's doing them as the moves are basically the same. So learn them the right way and keep doing them the right way. As long as you remain teachable and working on improving your skills, you'll have very a long career as a pro wrestler.

Some people get into pro wrestling thinking they'll be happy if they can have a good career on the indy scene. Seriously? Folks, I say this with great respect, but if that's all you want stay the hell out of pro wrestling.

I've heard many wrestling legends say, "Everyone who wants to get into pro wrestling should want to be champion. If you don't want to be champion, find something else to do." Basically what they're saying is either go big or go home. If you don't want to be the best, if you don't want to be world heavyweight champion, if you don't want to be at the top of the industry, then you're wasting your time and everybody else's time, and you should go do something else.

I can't emphasize this enough: You're trading your life to be in the wrestling industry, so why would you settle for anything less than being world champion?

I know a man who's wrestled hundreds of people, and has traveled many places for over 15 years. He's won championships, been in magazines, toured Japan, and has accomplished a great deal in his life. Yet, he feels that if he doesn't make it to WWE his career is a failure. I told him there are guys in WWE who haven't accomplished as much as he has in this industry, and no one can take that away from him.

I don't know if my words had any effect on him, but I felt I needed to say them to bring home a point: That there are tons of wrestlers who would kill to have his amazing career. If you're fortunate enough to get into the wrestling industry, go for it all. Keep pushing, keep trying, keep working hard, and you'll get there. But if all you want is a weekend hobby, go build model airplanes.

Competing for Promotion Spots

Now we come to the ugly side of pro wrestling: competing for spots. In every promotion there are "spots" (positions within the promotion as it relates to being a wrestler). For example, the main heavyweight champion has the top spot, the best bad guy has the top heel spot, and so on. When you get to the point where training tapers off, and you're working more shows on the road, the wrestlers will start to get competitive with each other.

Everybody wants the top spot, but only one person can have it. So guys will jockey for it or another important spot with the promoter, which happens everywhere in every promotion. When you get to that point, I'd suggest that rather than compete with other wrestlers for that one spot, create something unique that adds value to your gimmick. If you can make the promoter more money, they'll look at you in a more favorable way.

Why would I try to discourage you from competing? Because anything gained from competition can be lost through competition. When you create something that's unique to you, no one can take it away from you. Wrestling is a creative industry, so don't worry so much about spots and spend your time on developing your character and your gimmicks. Your abilities, professionalism, and passion for this business will become evident to your promoters and other wrestlers, and won't go unrewarded.

Drugs, Alcohol and the Ruination of Careers

You may have noticed that I haven't discussed the deaths that have occurred in wrestling as a result of alcohol and/or narcotics, because those cautionary tales have already been written by many others.

Also, it's not up to me to preach on the evils of alcohol and drugs since most of you already know about their ramifications. Suffice it to say, try to avoid pain killers wherever possible. Control yourself to only having two alcoholic drinks per week, and none is even better (alcohol turns to sugar, and if you're trying to be fit and healthy it's best not to imbibe).

I'm a realist about what goes on in the industry. I know people who like to drink, smoke pot, and snort coke once in a while, but they have great self-control and monitor themselves closely. Pot may not a big deal these days (especially with legalization in some states), but at the moment WWE still requires drug testing.

If you haven't done drugs previous to getting into pro wrestling, don't start as you'll need your body running at optimal efficiency 24/7 and 365 days a year. Promoters, bookers and trainers will notice your performance, so you may not have much of a career if you're more interested in being chemically altered and having fun at your expense.

What do you want more? To be high, or to be a champion? Of course the choice is yours. But just make sure you do all you can to not become another wrestling statistic.

CHAPTER 8: MYTHS EXPOSED!

There's a lot of conflicting information or misinformation about what you can realistically expect when you get into pro wrestling. As such, following are some myths of pro wrestling I'd like to dispel so you can have a better understanding of what you're getting into. I'm not listing these to crush your dreams, but so you don't get blindsided by things you were thought were true.

1. Since wrestling is "fake" you don't really get hurt.

FALSE. The moves, bumps, and overall ring action is **very** real because you can and probably will get hurt. So you should be prepared to live every day in some sort of pain (unfortunately, just like football or basketball players, the older you get the worse it can become), which is why wrestlers spend so much time in the indys honing their craft.

Photo Credit Euphoric Moments Photography

Wrestling can get pretty insane. Take it from XXX Lawrence Tyler as he demonstrates how to set a table on fire right before he puts someone through it!

Even seasoned veterans can botch a spot or move, and usually by accident. You have to keep improving on what you do to keep yourself and your "opponent" safe, so perfect practice makes perfect. I've seen guys get stretchered out, get concussions, and get busted open the hard way, so danger is always present.

2. Pro wrestling is like any other job where you get paid and get benefits.

VERY FALSE! Even if you're under contract you're an independent contractor, which means you agree to perform in promotions and they agree to pay you for your performance. However, they don't take federal, state or local taxes out of your pay. So you're responsible for keeping track of how much you get paid and all of your expenses, and retaining some of that money to pay taxes.

Sometimes you may get a 1099 tax form from a promotion, which is similar to a W-2 except it only lists what you were paid and no taxes are taken out. So you'll have to do the bookkeeping for that as well.

Also, you don't get benefits, so you'll have to purchase your own health insurance. Since wrestlers are considered high risk (meaning you'll use your insurance more than almost any other profession), you'll probably pay high premiums. If you don't have insurance and become injured, you'll have to pay the medical bill which can add up to a great deal of money over time.

If you have a relative or friend (or someone who may be referred to you) who's a doctor, you might want to see if you can work out some kind of payment plan with them. Anything you can do to save money is a plus, and the only way to minimize injury is to be solid in your ring work.

3. Once you become fully trained and start doing road shows, you'll be rich!

FALSE ... FALSE ... FALSE ... FALSE ... FALSE!
Here's the absolute truth: Unless you're a former WWE superstar working the indys, you won't get rich. Guys on the independent circuit work weekends for anywhere between $10 to $50 per match. Former superstars can command a higher payday because they've been to the Federation and people know them. Regular wrestlers who have a couple years in the industry may be making more, but that's because they do it full time. They go to promotions and wrestle, but they won't become rich.

Say you work four shows in one week including weekends, and you make $500. You think, *Great, I'm finally making good money!* However, you still have to pay for gas, food, hotel, your regular bills like your apartment rent, so $500 won't go very far. Receiving that amount of money is great, but you need to make sure you take care of all your financial obligations and save, save, save!

Talk to indy vets who can tell you the realities of being a pro wrestler so you know what you're getting into if you decide to stay in the industry. You **can** make it to the top as long as you understand it's up to you where you go and how you get there.

The good news is you won't necessarily have to do everything yourself, because there will be people to help you along the way. So be sure to listen to vets who are willing to advise and mentor you, and you'll be on your way to having a solid career in pro wrestling.

CONCLUSION

Pro wrestling is fun to watch, but it's even more fun to be involved in the industry.

Did I take my career as far as I thought it could go? Sadly, no. Am I bitter? Absolutely not, because I got to live my dream and not many people can say that. Most people are too afraid to go after their dreams, but I've been blessed that I got to do pretty much everything I ever wanted to do in wrestling (of course, with a lot of hard work and sometimes being in the right place at the right time).

I haven't had my WrestleMania moment yet, because I'm still working as a referee and am enjoying being a part of this incredible industry. I'm grateful for the time I've been able to spend as a pro wrestler, and all the awesome people I've had the pleasure of knowing and working with.

Plus, I'm grateful for the inspiration that told me to write this book. My hope is it will be handed down from one generation of wrestling hopefuls to another until the end of time. I believe my experiences can serve as advice as well as cautionary tales to people who want to wrestle but aren't sure what the wrestling world is like.

Reading the advice in these pages -- coupled with a reputable wrestling training school and your desire to be the best -- will give you the best shot possible at having a long, fulfilling and financially rewarding career in pro wrestling.

I wish you nothing but the best success!

Jeff "The Ref" Coles

GLOSSARY OF TERMS

Babyface (face): The hero or good guy.

Double Down: When both combatants are down on the mat and subject to the referee's 10 countdown.

Gassed: To be out of breath, tired, out of energy. Also known as "blown up." Example: "I'd get gassed just watching Warrior run to the ring!"

Gimmick: Probably the most overused word in wrestling because it can refer to so many things. For example:

- Your wrestling persona or character.
- A foreign object used by a wrestler or manager in a match.
- Merchandise for sale by wrestlers; usually t-shirts, DVDs, promo pictures.
- Gimmick tables and chairs that have been rigged to break on impact.

Heel: The villain or bad guy.

IWC: Internet Wrestling Community. These are mostly fan sites which include all the websites, forums and social media pages that report on the pro wrestling world.

Rest Hold: A hold used during a match which allows the wrestlers to catch their breath and rest for a few moments. Examples: Arm bar, reverse chin lock, body scissors.

Ring Rat: A female fan, similar to groupies of rock 'n roll, who hangs around after an event looking to hook up with one of the wrestlers.

Spots: A position with a promotion, or where you're in the pecking order of the promotion. Or a section of a match where multiple actions are taking place.

RESOURCES

Schools and Training Centers

Though I don't endorse any specific school (as I haven't gone to most), here are some of the more prominent wrestling schools and training centers. I haven't included the WWE Performance Center as you have to learn to crawl first, and WWE is for folks who are ready to run.

In the United States:

All Pro Wrestling (Dylan Drake, head trainer) Pacifica, CA
http://allprowrestling.com/boot-camp/#!

American Wrestling Federation (Ric Drasin) Sherman Oaks, CA
http://www.americanwrestlingfederation.com/Training.htm

Harley Race Wrestling Academy (Harley Race) Troy, MO
http://www.harleyrace.com

Larry Sharpe's Monster Factory (Danny Cage) Paulsboro, NJ
http://www.monsterfactory.org/about/

Ohio Valley Wrestling ("Nightmare" Danny Davis) Louisville, KY. Former WWE and TNA developmental center.
http://www.ovwrestling.com/training

Ring of Honor Dojo (Delerious) Bristol, PA
http://www.rohwrestling.com/content/ring-honor-dojo-0

Santino Brothers Wrestling School (Joey "KAOS" Munoz) Bell Gardens, CA
http://www.santinobros.net/newsdesk_info.php?newsdesk_id=77

Team 3D Academy (Bully Ray and D-Von) Kissimmee, FL
http://www.team3dacademy.com/

Wild Samoans Training Center (Afa Anoa'i) Minneola, FL
http://www.wswrestlingschool.com

WWA4 (Frank Aldridge) Atlanta, GA (You can see all of the people he's trained on the website.)
http://www.wwa4.com/

In Canada:

Hart Brothers University (Bruce and Ross Hart) Calgary, AB, Canada. At this time there's no website, so you'd have to write for information to:

>Hart Brothers Training Camp
>Suite #727, 105 - 150 Crowfoot Cr. N.W.
>Calgary, Alberta, Canada
>T3G 3T2

They also have a Facebook presence, which may be the best way to get your questions answered:
https://www.facebook.com/hartbrosuniversity

Pro Wrestling Canada (Moondog Manson) "Greater Vancouver Area, BC Canada"
http://www.prowrestlingcanada.com/dojo.php

Storm Wrestling Academy (Lance Storm) Calgary, AB, Canada
http://academy.stormwrestling.com/index1.html

Wrestling Gear

Following are a few sites where you can get wrestling trunks, tights, boots, kneepads, etc. Again, do your research as resources these days are all over the Internet:

Bizare Bazzar (Gear by Adrian Street):
http://www.bizarebazzar.com/

eLucha: http://elucha.com/products-elucha.php?idc=12

E-Z Money Tights: http://www.eztights.com/mainpage3.html
Highspots.com: http://highspots.com

Show-Off, Inc. (they also have dancing gear so don't get scared):
http://www.showoffinc.com/wrestling.htm
World Wrestling Gear: http://worldwrestlingwear.com/

The Warrior's 2014 Hall of Fame Acceptance Speech:

https://www.youtube.com/watch?v=huLa_WYwymY

WWE 2K14 Preorder Warrior Videogame Trailer

https://www.youtube.com/watch?v=iDmjBesg4-8

ABOUT THE AUTHOR

Photo Credit Euphoric Moments Photography

"I count to two...sometimes three..." ~ **Jeff "The Ref" Coles**

Jeff "The Ref" Coles has been involved in professional wrestling since 1985 as a fan, wrestler, manager, color commentator, ring announcer and wrestling referee.

For the last 23 years (since he was 20) he has literally walked the walk and talked the talk, and wrote ***Surviving the Ring***: ***Expert Advice for Getting in and Staying in the Tough World of Pro Wrestling*** to give you invaluable advice about the good, bad and the ugly of the tough world of pro wrestling.

There's no beating around the bush as he wants you to know the pros and cons of this maniacal (and often fun, sometimes profitable) industry:

"I wish I would have had this information available to me when I first started out. There's no getting around the fact that the world of pro wrestling is tough. There are a handful of people who are strong enough physically, mentally, and psychologically to make it a life-long career.

It's not about all the lights, gimmicks and media attention; it's a 24/7 lifestyle where these people become your family. If you're not committed to working harder than you've ever worked before, it might not be the career for you.

But hopefully the practical tips, tools, techniques I've learned over the years will help you make a well-informed decision about getting in and how to stay in this crazy world of professional wrestling that is like nothing else on earth!"

* * * * * * *

Jeff "The Ref" is currently working in Arizona with Honor Pro, the Arizona Wrestling Federation, and Lucha Libre Por (http://luchalibreusa.com/).

To contact him about his availability for national and international seminars, public speaking and referee bookings:

Email: bookjeffref@yahoo.com

You can also learn more about Jeff and the world of pro wrestling by following him on:

Facebook page: www.facebook.com/jefftheref37
Twitter: @REALJeffRef.

www.ingramcontent.com/pod-product-compliance
Lightning Source LLC
Chambersburg PA
CBHW042324150426
43192CB00001B/33